Switching on

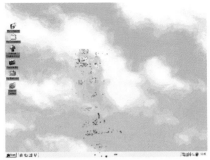

Your screen may have different pictures from this one.

The egg timer means that your computer is busy and wants you to wait.

1. You will need someone to help you the first time you switch the computer on. Ask them to tell you which buttons to press.

2. Wait for the screen to stop changing. It should have some small symbols on it and a pattern or picture in the background.

3. Whenever you see a small egg timer on your screen, your computer wants you to wait. Don't press any buttons until it goes away.

Holding your mouse

You give your computer instructions by pressing buttons on the mouse. Find out more about this on page 4.

Right-handers

Put your first finger on the left button.

Put your middle finger on the right button.

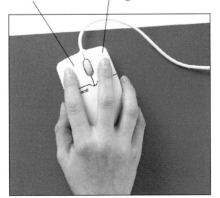

If you are right-handed, hold your mouse like this, with your first two fingers over the buttons.

Left-handers

Put your middle finger on the left button.

Put your first finger on the right button.

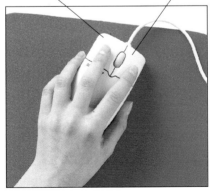

If you are left-handed, you may prefer to hold your mouse with your left hand, like this.

Switching off

You mustn't switch off your computer without shutting it down first. If you do, it may not work properly when you switch it back on. You can find out how to shut down on page 46.

3

Mouse doodles

These pages show you how to use the mouse to move an arrow, or pointer, on the screen. You can find out how to draw a big doodle like this one.

Clicking

Before you begin, try pressing the left button on your mouse, then lifting your finger up again. This is called clicking because the mouse makes a clicking sound.

Opening Paint

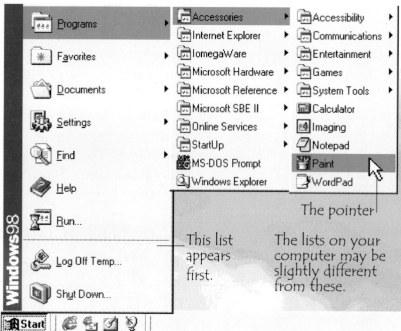

The pointer

This list appears first.

The lists on your computer may be slightly different from these.

1. To start, move the mouse until the pointer is in the bottom left-hand corner of your screen, over Start. Click on the left mouse button and a list appears.

2. Move the pointer up the list to Programs, then click the left mouse button. Move across to Accessories and click, then across and down to Paint. Click again.

4

The tool box

When you open Paint, you will find this tool box at the side of the screen. It contains all the tools you need to do different things in Paint.

Drawing

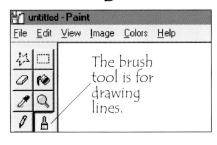

The brush tool is for drawing lines.

1. To draw a doodle, first move the mouse so the pointer is over the brush tool in the tool box. Click the left mouse button.

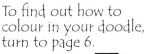

To find out how to colour in your doodle, turn to page 6.

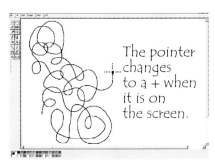

The pointer changes to a + when it is on the screen.

2. Move the pointer onto the screen. Keep your finger pressed down on the left mouse button all the time as you draw a wiggly line.

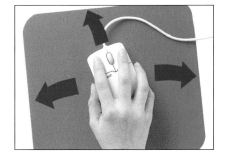

3. If the pointer disappears off the screen as you are drawing, just move the mouse around the mat until you can see it again.

Clear the screen

The Shift key

To clear the screen and start again, hold down the Ctrl and Shift keys on your keyboard at the same time. Then press the letter N.

5

Colouring in

On this page you can find out how to colour in the doodle you learned to draw on page 5. Try using the mouse to draw and colour some flowers, too.

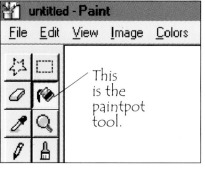

This is the paintpot tool.

This is the paint box.

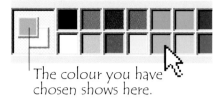

The colour you have chosen shows here.

1. To colour in a picture, move the mouse until the pointer is over the paintpot tool in the tool box. Click the left mouse button.

2. Move the pointer onto a colour you like in the paint box. The paint box is at the bottom of the screen. Click the left mouse button.

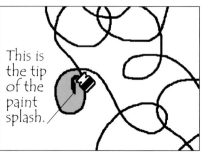

This is the tip of the paint splash.

Fill your doodle with different colours.

3. Move the pointer onto the screen. It changes to a paintpot. Put the tip of the paint splash on the area you want to colour in, and click.

4. To fill another area with a different colour, choose another colour in the paint box and click on it. Click on the doodle.

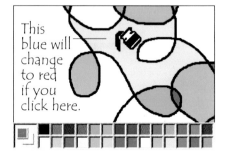

This blue will change to red if you click here.

5. It is easy to change a colour in your picture. Just click on a different colour in the paint box, then click on top of the first colour.

Internet link: For a link to a website where you can experiment with lines, shapes and colours to create pictures online, go to **www.usborne-quicklinks.com**

Flowers

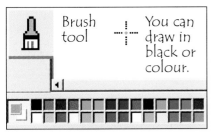

Brush tool

You can draw in black or colour.

Don't leave any gaps in your outline or the colour will leak out.

1. To draw a flower, click on the brush tool in the tool box. Click on black or a colour in the paint box. Put the pointer on the screen.

2. Hold the left mouse button down and move the mouse to draw the middle of a flower. Add some petals. Colour the flower in.

Spraying colour

This is the airbrush tool.

Hold your finger down on the mouse button for strong colour.

This blob gives the biggest spray.

1. To make colour look as if it has been sprayed on, you can use a tool called the airbrush. Click on the spray can in the tool box.

2. A box appears below the tool box. Click on a blob in this box to choose the size of the spray. Put the pointer on the screen and click.

These flowers were done with the airbrush tool.

Made a mistake?

Press here.

Clicking here would change the colour of the line.

If you make a mistake, before you do anything else, hold down the Ctrl key, then press the letter Z. This will undo the mistake.

It is easy to change the colour of an outline by mistake when you are colouring in. Just press Ctrl and Z to undo the mistake.

7

Drawing lines

Here you can use your mouse to do some more drawing and colouring. You will find out how to draw snails like these and how to draw straight lines, too. First, make sure Paint is open (see page 4).

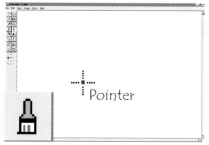

Paint box

Draw eyes with the brush tool.

1. Click on the brush tool in the tool box. Then click on a colour you like in the paint box. Move the pointer onto the screen.

2. Hold the left mouse button down and draw around and around to make a shell. Add a body, feelers and a mouth.

3. Draw dots for eyes by clicking once, then moving the mouse. Colour your snail using the paintpot and paint box.

This snail has been drawn with the thickest brush (see page 9).

To give a picture a coloured background, click in any space with the paintpot, when the picture is finished.

Thick or thin?

When you click on the brush tool, a box appears below the tool box. You can use it to choose the type or thickness of line you draw.

Click on different symbols for different looks.

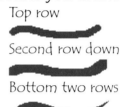

Top row

Second row down

Bottom two rows

Click on a symbol in the right-hand row to draw a thin line.

Click on a symbol in the middle row to draw a medium line.

Click on a symbol in the left-hand row to draw a thick line.

Straight lines

 This is the line tool.

Thinnest line

This line has been clicked on.

Thickest line

1. To draw straight lines, you can use a tool called the line tool. Click on the line tool in the tool box.

2. A box appears below the tool box. Click on a line in this box to choose how thick a line to draw.

If your line looks jagged like this, move the mouse very slightly until it is straighter.

Can you draw a brick for a snail to sit on?

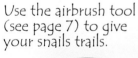

Use the airbrush tool (see page 7) to give your snails trails.

3. Put the pointer on the screen. Hold down the left mouse button and move the mouse to draw a line. Lift your finger.

Put the pointer at the back of a snail. Hold the left mouse button down and draw a wiggly trail.

4. It may take practice to get your lines to join up with one another properly. (To find out how to rub out, see page 17.)

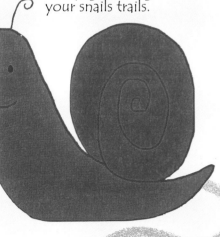

Drawing shapes

There are four tools in the tool box for drawing shapes. Open Paint and you will find them at the bottom of the tool box.

Rectangle tool

Paintbox

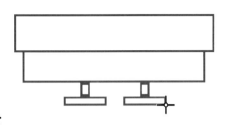

Draw rectangles like these.

Draw squares or rectangles with this tool.

Draw any shape with this odd-shape tool.

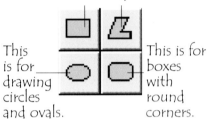

This is for drawing circles and ovals.

This is for boxes with round corners.

1. To draw a space buggy similar to the one on page 11, first click on the rectangle tool and then on a colour in the paint box.

2. Hold the left mouse button down and move the mouse down and to one side to draw a rectangle. Add more rectangles.

Thick or thin?

To draw shapes with thick outlines, first click on the line tool, above the shape tools. Then, click on a thick line in the box below the tool box. Finally, click on a shape tool and draw a shape.

Line tool

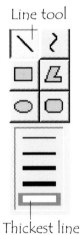

Thickest line

It can be best to draw and colour things such as wheels separately, then move them to where you want them (see page 12).

Use the brush tool to draw clouds and exhaust fumes.

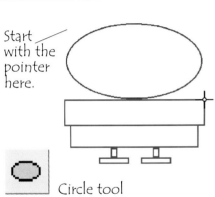

Start with the pointer here.

Circle tool

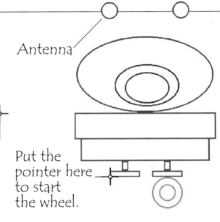

Antenna

Put the pointer here to start the wheel.

Odd shapes

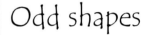

Odd-shape tool

3. Click on the circle tool and a colour, then put the pointer above and to one side of the rectangles. Draw an oval as shown above.

4. Draw more ovals and circles in whatever colours you like for the space man's helmet and face, and for the wheels and antennae.

1. Click on the odd-shape tool, then draw a line. Lift your finger and put the pointer somewhere else on the screen.

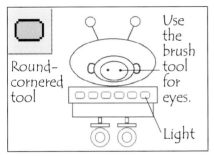

Round-cornered tool

Use the brush tool for eyes.

Light

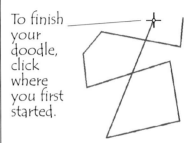

To finish your doodle, click where you first started.

5. Use the round-cornered tool to add "ears" to the helmet and to draw the buggy's lights. Don't worry if these are not exactly alike.

6. Click on the line tool and draw the space man's nose and neck. Finish the antennae and add a spark. Colour your picture.

2. Click the mouse. A new line will join up with the first. Continue doing this until you have drawn a doodle.

Moving and stretching

When you have drawn a picture, you may want to move it to another place on your screen. These pages show you how to do this and how to change your pictures by stretching and shrinking them.

Moving a picture

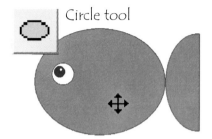

Circle tool

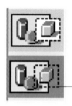

This is the select tool.

Click here, or you won't be able to make one picture overlap another.

1. Use the circle tool to draw a fish's body and an eye. Add a tail with the brush and line tools. Then, colour the fish in.

2. Click on the dotted box at the top of the tool box. This is the select tool. Then, click on the bottom box which appears below the tool box.

Start with the pointer here.

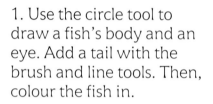

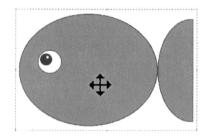

3. Put the pointer above and to one side of the fish. Hold the left button down and move the mouse to draw a box right around it.

4. When you lift your finger up, the pointer changes. It becomes a different kind of cross. Move this cross so it is inside the dotted box.

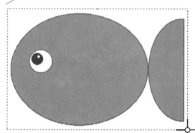

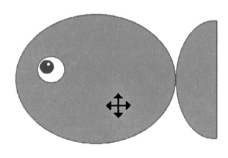

5. Hold the left button down and move the mouse to drag the fish to a new spot. Click outside the box to make the box disappear.

Changing shape

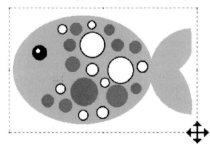

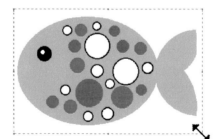

1. To stretch or shrink a picture, click on the select tool and the bottom box below the tool box. Draw a box around the picture.

2. Move the cross to any one of the tiny squares around the edge of the box. Put it exactly on top. The cross changes to an arrow.

Drag the arrow out to stretch your fish.

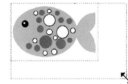

Move the arrow in to make the fish smaller.

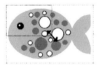

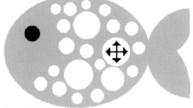

This fish lost its coloured spots when it was stretched.

This fish has been stretched longways.

3. Hold the left mouse button down and drag the arrow away from your picture to stretch it, or onto it to shrink it.

4. Your picture may lose some of its colour when you change its shape. Try moving it and the colour should come back.

This fish has been stretched sideways.

13

Making more space

If you want to draw a big picture, you may need to make more space on your screen. Here are some quick and easy ways to do this. If you want to draw a picture to fill a sheet of A4 paper when you print it out, read pages 28 and 29 as well.

You may need to make more space to draw a big picture like the one on this screen.

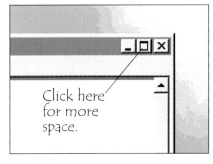

Click here for more space.

1. Look for a square symbol near the top right of your Paint screen. Click on it. This may give you more space for drawing.

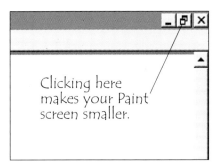

Clicking here makes your Paint screen smaller.

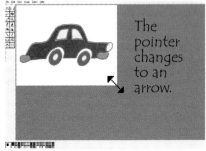

The pointer changes to an arrow.

2. If you see the symbol shown above at the top right of your screen, clicking on it will make your Paint screen smaller, not bigger.

3. If step 1 doesn't work, look for tiny squares around your drawing area. Put your pointer exactly on the square at the bottom right.

4. When the pointer changes, press the left mouse button and drag the arrow down and right. This gives you more space to draw.

14

Internet link: *For a link to a website where you can colour in a scene, go to* **www.usborne-quicklinks.com**

Moving around

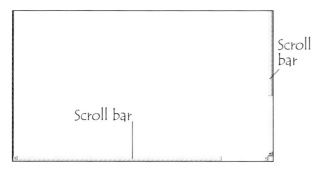

Scroll bar

Scroll bar

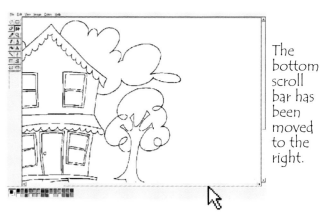

The bottom scroll bar has been moved to the right.

1. You may have bars on two edges of your screen. These are called scroll bars. You can use them to give you more space to draw.

2. When your screen is full, put the pointer on the bottom scroll bar, press the left mouse button and drag the bar to the right.

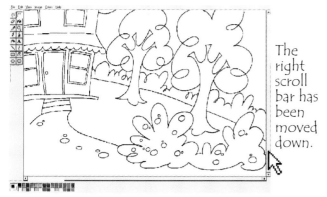

The right scroll bar has been moved down.

The bottom bar has been moved to the left.

3. Now you can add things to the right of your picture. To draw below it as well, drag the right-hand scroll bar down.

4. To see the left edge of your picture again, drag the bottom scroll bar to the left. Now you can fill in the bottom left-hand corner.

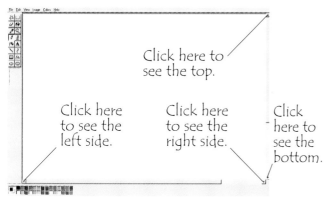

Click here to see the top.

Click here to see the left side.

Click here to see the right side.

Click here to see the bottom.

5. Another way of moving the scroll bars is to click on the arrows shown above. If it is easier, move around the screen this way.

6. You can't see all of your picture at once when you are using scroll bars. To do this, you have to print it out (see pages 30-31).

15

Drawing details

As you get better at using Paint, you might want to draw more detailed pictures. Here are some tips to help you. Try using them to draw details on a clown, like the one below. It is easier to draw details if you zoom in on the area you want to work on.

Zooming in

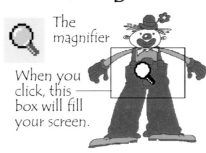

The magnifier

When you click, this box will fill your screen.

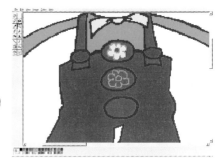

1. Click on the magnifier in the tool box. Put the magnifier over the area you want to zoom in on. Click the left mouse button.

2. The picture enlarges. Now you can use the drawing tools to add some details, for example, flowers on the clown's buttons.

Internet link: For a link to a website where you can read about some famous portraits and find useful tips for drawing your own portraits, go to **www.usborne-quicklinks.com**

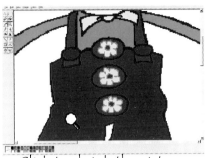
Click to shrink the picture.

Drag to the top to move your picture down.

Drag to move the picture right.

Using pencil

Pencil tool

3. To get your picture back to normal size, click on the magnifier in the tool box again, then click anywhere on the screen.

4. Your picture may have moved. To get it back into position, drag the bottom scroll bar to the left and the right scroll bar to the top.

You might like to use the pencil tool for drawing some details. The pencil is the same thickness as the thinnest brush.

Brush colouring

Colour small areas with the brush.

Dead straight

Line tool

You can draw lines like these perfectly straight.

If you have a very small area to colour in, it can be easier to use the brush tool, instead of the paintpot.

1. You can draw some lines perfectly straight by using the line tool and the Shift key on the keyboard as well.

2. Hold down the Shift key while you draw a line. Lift your finger off the mouse before you take it off Shift.

Rubbing out

Eraser tool

Click here to rub out small details.

Click here to rub out large areas.

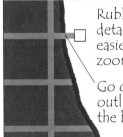
Rubbing out details is easier if you zoom in first.

Go over the outline with the brush tool.

1. To rub out a mistake, click on the eraser tool. Click on a square in the box below the tool box to choose an eraser size.

2. A square appears on the screen. Move it over the area you want to rub out, holding down the left mouse button.

17

Copying a picture

You can make copies of the things you draw. The cats on these pages were all copied from one original cat. Then the colours were changed. The mice were done in the same way.

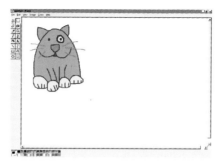

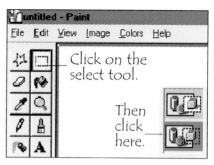

Click on the select tool.

Then click here.

1. Draw and colour a cat like this one with the brush and paintpot tools. Try not to make it too big, as you will need space to copy it.

2. Click on the select tool at the top of the tool box. Then, click on the bottom box of shapes which appears below the tool box.

Once you have made your copies, you can move them to wherever you want them (see pages 12 and 21).

3. Put the pointer above and to the left-hand side of the cat. Draw a box which goes all the way around the cat, as shown above.

4. Put the cross inside the dotted box. Hold down the Ctrl key, then press the left mouse button. Start to move the mouse.

5. Another cat will appear as you move the mouse. Drag the new cat well away from the first one, then lift your fingers.

6. To make another copy straightaway, again hold down the Ctrl key, then press the left mouse button and move the mouse.

More about rubbing out

The eraser tool (see page 17) is useful for rubbing out small parts of a picture that go wrong, for example, a mouse's tail.

To rub out a whole mouse, it is easier just to draw a box around it with the select tool, then press the Delete key on the keyboard.

Turning a picture

You can turn your pictures around if you want to. The bees on these pages were first copied and then some were turned. Some were stretched or shrunk, too.

Click here to turn the bee upside down.

Click here and the bee will turn back to front.

Click here and the bee will do a quarter turn.

Select tool

Click here.

1. Draw and colour a bee. Then make a few copies of it (see pages 18-19). Make sure that each bee has space for a box around it.

2. To make a bee turn, first click on the select tool and the bottom box below the tool box. Draw a box right around the bee.

3. Hold down Ctrl and press the letter R. A box appears, like the one above. Click on a circle in the box, then on OK. Your bee will turn.

Draw a flower, then make lots of copies of it.

Stretch and shrink some bees and flowers.

Move the bees and flowers to wherever you want them.

20

Crowded screen?

There are lots of times when you need to draw a box around something with the select tool. Often you don't have room, because the box bumps into something else. Below you can find out how to use a different select tool instead.

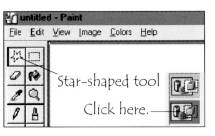

Star-shaped tool

Click here.

1. The other select tool you can use is the star-shaped tool. Click on it in the tool box, and on the bottom box below the tool box.

2. Put the pointer close to a bee and carefully draw a line around it. A box will appear when you lift your finger off the mouse.

Fill the flowers with different colours.

3. With the star-shaped tool, it doesn't matter that the box overlaps the flower. You can now make your bee do what you want it to.

To move the bee, press the left mouse button and drag.

4. You can move your bee, stretch, shrink, copy or delete it, all in the usual way. You can't turn it using the star-shaped tool, though.

Using white

Use the paintpot to make the wings white again.

White becomes transparent when you move it on top of something else. Colour your bees' wings white once the bees are in position.

21

Dragging shapes

You can drag shapes or pictures you have drawn around the screen to make special effects, like the ones on these pages.

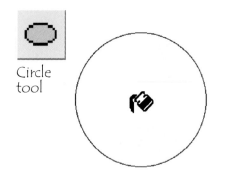

Circle tool

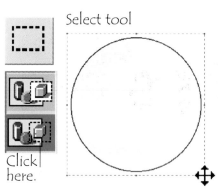

Select tool

Click here.

1. Draw a circle in one colour on the left of your screen. Then fill it with a different colour, using the paintpot tool.

2. Click on the select tool and on the bottom box of shapes below the tool box. Draw a box which goes right around your circle.

Shift key

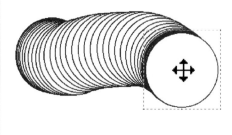

3. Move the cross so that it is inside the dotted box. Press Shift on the keyboard, then hold the left mouse button down.

4. Keeping both fingers held down, drag the cross around the screen. A line of circles will appear. Lift your fingers to finish.

Adding patterns

Try adding a face, feet and two antennae to an oval shape.

You can add patterns to a shape before you drag it. Simple patterns using just a few colours work best.

Octopus

Fill the head with the same colour as the outline.

1. Draw the outline of a head with the brush tool. Fill it in with the same colour, using the paintpot. Add eyes and a mouth.

2. Draw a circle in another part of the screen. Draw a box around it, using the select tool. Move it to the bottom of the head.

3. Holding down the Shift key, drag the circle away from the head to make a tentacle. Make seven more tentacles in the same way.

Fast and slow

If you move your mouse fast, the shapes are spaced out.

If you move your mouse slowly, they are close together.

The faster you move your mouse when you are dragging, the further apart your shapes will be.

23

Adding words

You can use the Paint program for writing as well as for drawing pictures. It is best to use Paint if you only want to add a few words to a picture, such as your name and a title. If you want to do a lot of writing, you will need to use the WordPad program instead. You can find out all about WordPad on pages 38-43.

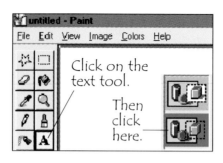

1. To write in Paint, you need to use the text (words) tool. Click on the text tool and the bottom box of shapes below the tool box.

2. In a space on the screen, hold the left mouse button down and move the mouse down and to one side to draw a box for your words.

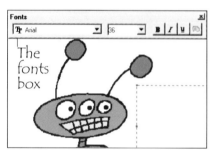

3. A new box called Fonts may appear at the top of your screen. This lets you change the look and size of the words you write.

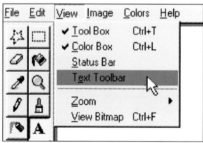

4. If the box doesn't appear, click on View at the top left of your screen, then on Text Toolbar. The fonts box will appear.

5. Click in the text box and type some words on the keyboard. They will appear in the text box. There are some tips to help you below.

Typing tips

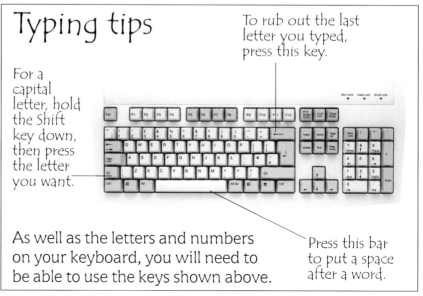

For a capital letter, hold the Shift key down, then press the letter you want.

To rub out the last letter you typed, press this key.

Press this bar to put a space after a word.

As well as the letters and numbers on your keyboard, you will need to be able to use the keys shown above.

Changing size

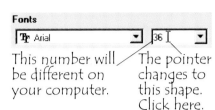

This number will be different on your computer.

The pointer changes to this shape. Click here.

robot

Your words change to the size you have typed. This is size 26.

This is size 65.

1. If your words are too big for the box, or too small to read, move the pointer to the fonts box. Click in the box with the number in it.

2. To make your words smaller, type a smaller number than the one in the fonts box. Put the pointer back in the text box. Click.

3. To make words bigger, type a bigger number than is in the fonts box, then click in the text box. Numbers from 26 to 72 will look best.

Watch out!

The text and fonts boxes disappear.

If you click anywhere outside the text box or fonts box, your words become "fixed". You can't easily alter them any more.

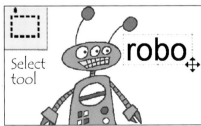

Select tool

If you do this by mistake before you have finished, draw a box around the words with the select tool, press Delete and start again.

Changing words

On pages 24-25 you learned to type words in Paint and make them the size you want. Here you can find out how to change the look of words in other ways. Don't click outside the text or fonts box until you are happy with your words.

You can type words in black or colour. To change colour, just click on a new colour in the paintbox.

This word is italic.

This is bold.

The word below is bold, italic and underlined.

All the words above are in a font called Times New Roman.

Which look?

Click here.

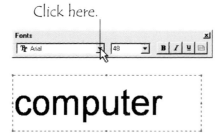

1. Click on the text tool, draw a text box, and type some words (see page 24). Click on the arrow shown above in the fonts box.

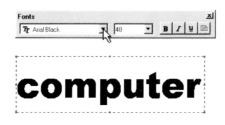

3. The name appears at the top of the fonts box and the look of your words changes. To get the list back, click on the arrow again.

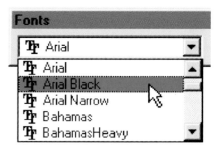

2. A list of names appears. These are type styles, or fonts. Some computers have more than others. Put the pointer on a name and click.

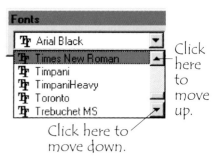

Click here to move up.

Click here to move down.

4. You can move up and down the list by clicking on the arrows beside it. Click on different names to see which style you like best.

Adding extras

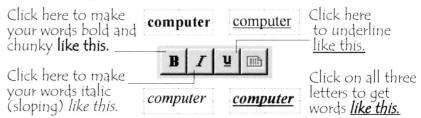

Click here to make your words bold and chunky **like this.**

Click here to make your words italic (sloping) *like this.*

Click here to underline like this.

Click on all three letters to get words ***like this.***

Another way to change the look of words is by clicking on the letters shown above. These are on the right of the fonts box.

To change words back to how they were before, click on the same letter again. To get rid of underlining, for example, click on U again.

Correcting mistakes

moose

A flashing line appears when you click.

mouse

A coloured background appears when you double click.

cat and dog

Remember, don't click outside the text box until you've finished.

1. If you realize that a letter in a word is wrong, put the pointer on the left of the letter and click. Press Delete and type the correct letter.

2. To change a whole word, put the pointer anywhere on the word and double click (see page 28). Type a new word or press Delete.

3. If you have missed out a letter or a space, put the pointer where it should go and click. Type the letter or press the space bar.

Bigger box

hippopota mus

hippopotamus

Drag to the right until the word fits.

Instead of making words smaller to fit in a text box, you can stretch the box, if you have room. Follow steps 2 and 3 on page 13.

Into position

Use the select tool to move your words to a new position.

Select tool

amy

Once you have clicked outside the text box, you can do to your words the things you normally do in Paint, such as move them.

Ciao

This font is called Nueva MM.

Guten Tag

Bike DT

Dag

FC_Icone

Salut

Garamond

Hi

Benguiat

Buongiorno

Bonjour

Lucida Handwriting

Tempus Sans ITC

This is Wingdings™. It has symbols instead of letters.

27

Filling a page

Here you can find out how to draw a big picture which will fill a sheet of A4 paper when you print it out. Your printer will always leave a border around the edge of your picture.

A wide picture will fill the page like this, when you print it on A4 paper.

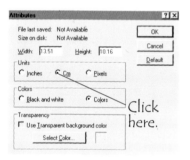

Click here.

1. To draw a wide picture to fill a sheet of A4 paper, first press Ctrl and E on the keyboard. A box appears. Click on the circle by Cm.

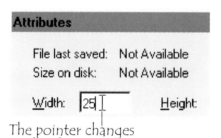

The pointer changes to this shape.

2. Move the pointer into the Width box and double click (see below). Type 25 on the keyboard. The number 25 appears in the box.

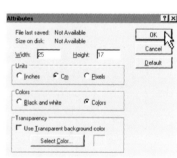

3. Move the pointer into the Height box and double click. Type 17. This appears in the box. Click on OK. The box disappears.

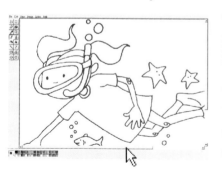

4. Start drawing on the left of your screen. When you reach the right edge, drag the bottom scroll bar to go wider (see page 15).
28

5. To go lower as well, drag down the scroll bar on the right, as shown above. To see the left edge again, move the bottom bar left.

Double clicking

You know you have double clicked properly when a coloured background appears.

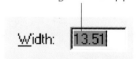

To double click, just click the left mouse button twice very fast. Keep the mouse still and only press lightly when you do this.

Tall pictures

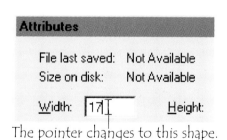

The pointer changes to this shape.

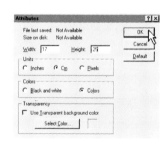

1. To draw a tall picture to fill a sheet of A4 paper, first press Ctrl and E. When a box appears, click on the circle by Cm.

2. Move the pointer into the Width box and double click (see page 28). Type 17 on the keyboard. The number 17 appears in the box.

3. Move the pointer into the Height box and double click. Type 25. This appears in the box. Click on OK. The box disappears.

Your picture will fill an A4 page like this when you print it out.

4. Start drawing at the top of your screen. When you reach the bottom, use the scroll bar on the right to go lower (see page 15).

5. If the bottom scroll bar is showing, you can go wider too. Your picture will fill an A4 page lengthways when you print it out.

Printing

If you have a printer for your computer, you can print your pictures out onto paper. First of all, switch on the printer and put some A4 paper in it. You may need someone to help you with this. Then, there are a few things you need to check before you print.

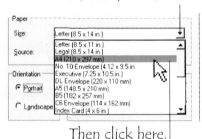

Ready to print?

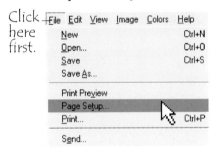

Click here first.

1. Click on File in the top left-hand corner of your screen. A list appears. Move the pointer down the list to Page Setup and click.

2. A big box like this one appears. This will let you choose which way round you want your picture to print on the paper.

Click on this arrow first.

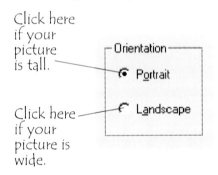

Then click here.

3. Look at the Paper Size part of the box. Does it say A4? If not, click on the arrow shown above. Then click on A4 in the list.

Check the fit

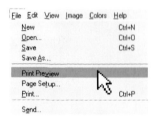

1. To see how your picture will fit on the paper, click on File. Then, click on Print Preview in the list.
30

Click here if your picture is tall.

Click here if your picture is wide.

4. If your picture is a fairly tall shape, click on the circle by Portrait. If your picture is wide, click on Landscape. Click on OK.

A picture to be printed portrait.

A picture to be printed landscape.

2. Your picture appears on paper. Check that it fits, then click on Close at the top of the screen.

Portrait   Landscape

You can cut off any spare paper.

5. If your picture is fairly small, or square, it may not matter whether you click on Portrait or Landscape. It will fit the paper either way.

This picture is too tall for landscape. Click on Portrait (see step 4).

This is too wide for portrait. Click on Landscape.

3. If part of your picture looks chopped off the paper, check that you followed all the instructions above.

Internet link: For a link to a website where you can print pictures to make into a flipbook, go to www.usborne-quicklinks.com

Print out

When you are sure you are ready to print, hold down Ctrl and press P on the keyboard. A box like this appears. Click on OK. Your picture will print out.

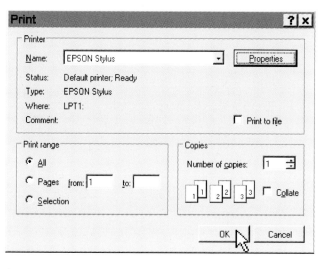

Hand colouring

If you print out a picture without colouring it in on screen first, you can then colour it in on paper with felt-tip pens or crayons.

Quick print

A colour picture can take a long time to print and uses a lot of ink. It is a good idea to do a quick test print in black and white first.

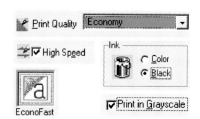

After you have pressed Ctrl and P, click on Properties in the Print box. Then, look for words like the ones above to click on and OK.

31

Making cards

The easiest way to make a card is first to draw and print out a picture, then cut the picture out and glue it onto a piece of thin card. You will need to print onto white paper or the colours will look very dull. If you don't want your background to be white, you can colour it in on screen before you print the picture out.

What size?

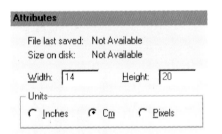

To make sure your picture isn't too big to fit on A4 card, follow steps 1, 2 and 3 on page 29, but type 14 for the width, 20 for the height.

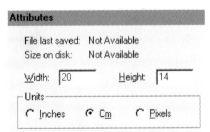

If you want to draw a wide picture and fold your card like the snowmen one on page 33, type 20 for the width, 14 for the height.
32

Cutting a card

Measure and cut out a piece of card twice as big as your picture. Fold the card in half and glue the picture on the front.

Lots of copies

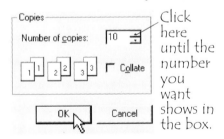

Click here until the number you want shows in the box.

You may want to print several copies of a picture for, say, Christmas cards. After pressing Ctrl and P, click in the Copies box.

Birthday cake

1. Use the circle tool to draw a wide oval for the cake top. Draw candles with the line or rectangle tool and flames with the pencil or brush.

2. Use the eraser tool to rub out the lines inside each candle. You'll find it easier if you zoom in first with the magnifier (see page 16).

3. Use the pencil or brush to draw the icing and the rest of the cake. Colour the cake in. Zoom in to do this if it is easier.

Yellow has leaked from the flame into the background. Fill in the gap with pencil or brush.

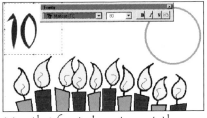

Use the fonts box to get the font and size you want.

You can make cards of different shapes and sizes.

4. If colour leaks out of one area into another, press Ctrl and Z to undo the mistake, then look for gaps in your lines. Fill in the gaps.

5. Draw a circle to put the age in. In a space, type the age using the text tool, then move it into the circle. Colour in the background.

You can leave a border of card around your pictures.

33

Wrapping paper

You can use Paint to make your own wrapping paper and matching gift tags. The present must be small enough to be wrapped in A4 paper, though. First, follow steps 1, 2 and 3 on page 29, so that you can fill the paper with your design.

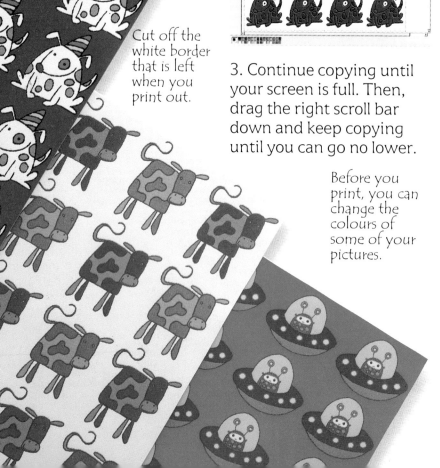

You can add a background colour before you print.

Cut off the white border that is left when you print out.

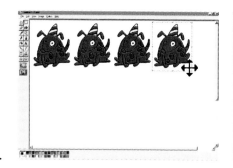

1. Draw a small picture in the top left-hand corner of your screen. Make copies of it (see pages 18-19) and arrange them in a row.

2. Draw a box around the whole row of pictures with the select tool. Copy the row to make a second row below the first.

3. Continue copying until your screen is full. Then, drag the right scroll bar down and keep copying until you can go no lower.

4. If the bottom scroll bar is showing, drag it to the right. Draw a box around some pictures as shown above. Copy them into the space.

Before you print, you can change the colours of some of your pictures.

5. Drag the right scroll bar toward the top of the screen and keep copying pictures until you have filled the whole area.

Gift tags

The sticky side

You can make a gift tag in the same way as a card (see page 32). Put some folded sticky tape on the back and press it onto the present.

Shrinking and stretching

Leave enough space to draw a box around the picture.

Delete all the pictures but one. Stretch the one that's left.

If you find it hard to draw a picture small enough for your paper or gift tag, draw it bigger instead, then shrink it (see page 13).

Or, you may want to stretch a small picture from your wrapping paper to make a matching gift tag. Print out the paper first.

Fun with letters

You can create designs with letters in Paint to make all kinds of things. Try experimenting with different looks and sizes of letters. You could make a nameplate for the door of your room, name stickers for your friends to wear at a party, or bookmarks to give to people.

Nameplate

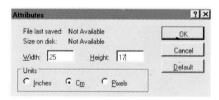

1. To make your nameplate a wide shape, follow steps 1 to 3 on page 28. Your name will run across the paper when you print it.

2. Click on the text tool in the toolbox. Draw a deep, wide text box going right across your screen. Type your name.

3. Use the fonts box to change the style and size of your letters. Look at pages 25 and 26 if you can't remember how to do this.

4. You can then add a border with the rectangle tool. Colour in your letters and the border using the paintpot tool.

Draw a picture next to your name.

For spots, use the brush tool. Click once for each spot.

Internet link: For a link to a website where you can print a story and make it into a book, go to **www.usborne-quicklinks.com**

Party stickers

Sticky-backed paper is usually A4 size.

1. You will need to buy some sheets of sticky-backed paper if you want to print name stickers for people to wear.

2. Follow steps 1 to 3 on page 29, so you can fill an A4 sheet. You will probably fit between six and eight stickers on one sheet.

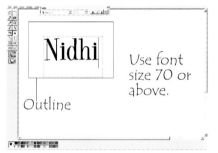

Outline

Use font size 70 or above.

3. To make a sticker, first draw an outline with a shape tool or the brush tool. Use the text tool and fonts box to do the name.

4. Decorate the sticker with a pattern or picture and fill the background. Make a whole sheet of stickers and print them out.

Cut out the stickers when they are printed.

Bookmarks

Do each letter separately.

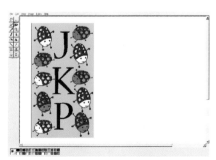

1. Draw a bookmark shape with the rectangle tool. Use the text tool to do someone's initials. Position them on the bookmark.

2. Decorate the bookmark and colour the background. Print the bookmark, then cut it out and glue it onto a piece of card.

More about words

On the next six pages you can find out how to do some writing on your computer, using the program WordPad. Learn how to add pictures to your writing to make an invitation, or illustrate a letter, story or poem. You will need to do some of the same things you do when you are writing in Paint. You may need to look back at pages 24-27 to remind you of these.

Opening WordPad

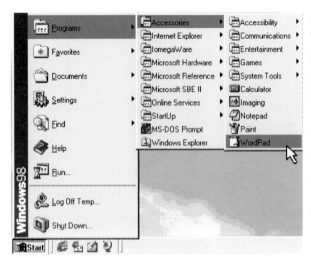

Opening WordPad is similar to opening Paint. Click on Start, move up the list to Programs, across to Accessories, then across and down to WordPad. Click the left mouse button.

Typing words

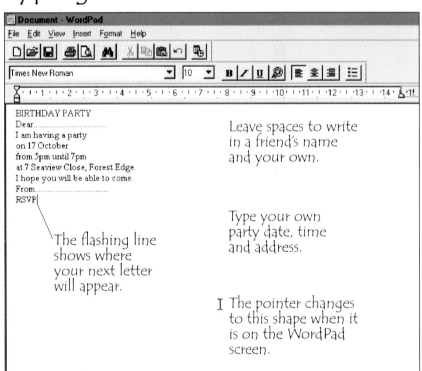

BIRTHDAY PARTY
Dear.................
I am having a party
on 17 October
from 5pm until 7pm
at 7 Seaview Close, Forest Edge.
I hope you will be able to come.
From...............
RSVP

The flashing line shows where your next letter will appear.

Leave spaces to write in a friend's name and your own.

Type your own party date, time and address.

I The pointer changes to this shape when it is on the WordPad screen.

The WordPad screen appears. To learn how to use WordPad, try making an invitation similar to the one on page 39.

Type what you would say for your invitation. Look at Typing tips on pages 24 and 39, and Correcting mistakes on page 27 if you need to.

Start a new line

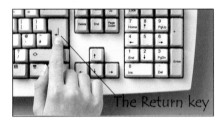
The Return key

To start a new line when you are typing, press this large key on the keyboard. It is called Return.

Dotted lines

Dear .... Maria

To do a dotted line so that you can write in someone's name, hold your finger down on the full stop key until the line is long enough.

Internet link: For a link to a website where you can find out the meaning of words and have fun writing poems, go to **www.usborne-quicklinks.com**

More typing tips

You will need to use some extra keys on the keyboard, now you are typing more words.

! For an exclamation mark, hold down Shift and press this key.

" To do speech marks, hold down Shift and press this key.

The Return key

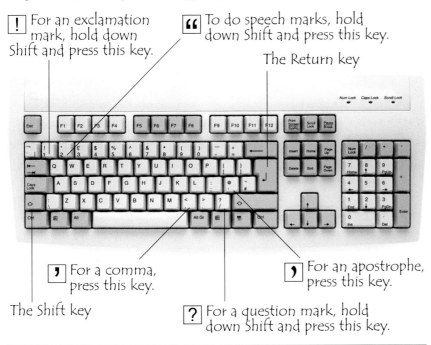

The Shift key

, For a comma, press this key.

' For an apostrophe, press this key.

? For a question mark, hold down Shift and press this key.

BIRTHDAY PARTY

Dear ....

I am having a party
on 17 October
from 5pm until 7pm
at 7 Seaview Close, Forest Edge.
I hope you will be able to come.

From ....

RSVP

Spacing out

Click and press Return for a line space.

To make a space between two lines of text, put the pointer at the end of the first line, click and press the Return key.

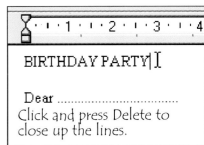

Click and press Delete to close up the lines.

If you ever need to close up two lines of text, put the pointer at the end of the first line, click, then press Delete on the keyboard.

On these invitations, a line space has been made after the word PARTY and after From............

On the next two pages you can find out how to position your words on an invitation and how to add pictures to it.

39

More about changing words

Whenever you want to change the look of words in WordPad, you first have to select, or highlight, them. Have a practice at doing this by following steps 1 to 5. Then you can make the changes to your invitation suggested below.

PARTY

1. Select a single word by double clicking on it. When a word is selected, it gets a coloured background.

II am having a party

2. To select more than one word, put your pointer at the start of the first word. Press the left mouse button.

I am having a party

3. Keeping the mouse button held down all the time, drag the pointer along the line of words from left to right.

I am having a party on 17 October

4. To select more than one line, keep your finger held down at the end of the first line and drag the pointer down onto the next line.

I am having a party on 17 October

Click anywhere to deselect.

5. To get rid of highlighting, just click anywhere on the screen. This is called deselecting. You have to do this after making changes.

Centring

This is the centring symbol.

The words are now centred.

To centre your words on the page, first select them all, then click on the centring symbol shown above. Click anywhere to deselect.

40

Changing size and look

For changing size

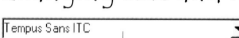

The fonts box

Palette symbol for changing colour.

Try size 12 for the main part of your invitation.

Click here first.

First select your words. Then, use the fonts box to change their size and style, as you did on pages 25 and 26. Click to deselect.

To change a word's colour, select it, then click on the palette symbol in the fonts box. Click on a colour in the list, then click to deselect.

Words and pictures

When your words are finished, you can put them into Paint and add some pictures. Here's how you do this.

If you give your invitation a coloured background, fill the insides of the letters with the same colour afterwards.

You can try designing notices and posters, too.

1. Select all the words you have written in WordPad (see page 40). Hold down the Ctrl key and then press C. Open Paint.

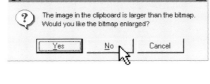

2. Hold down Ctrl, then press V. If this message appears, click on No. Your words will appear with a dotted box around them.

3. Put the cross inside the box, then press the left mouse button and drag the words to exactly where you want them.

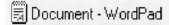

Look for this bar at the bottom of your screen.

4. If the words are too big, press Delete. Click on this bar at the bottom of your screen. Your words will appear in WordPad again.

Look for this bar at the bottom of your screen.

5. Use the fonts size box to make the words smaller. Press Ctrl and C. Click on the bar shown above. Repeat steps 2 and 3.

6. Click on one of the drawing tools in the tool box and draw whatever pictures you want to complete your invitation.

41

Writing on your computer

You can use WordPad as you did on pages 38-40 if you want to do a longer piece of writing, such as a story, letter or poem. Here are some extra tips to help you. You can find out how to add a picture to your writing, too, and how to get ready to print out. First, open WordPad.

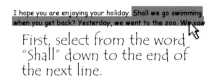

Choose a font and size you can read easily, such as Comic Sans MS, size 14.

1. If you are going to do a lot of writing, it can be best to choose a font and size before you start.

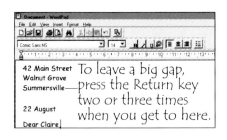

To leave a big gap, press the Return key two or three times when you get to here.

2. Write your story, letter or poem following the instructions you were given on pages 38-40.

Moving words

Imagine you want to move this sentence.

I hope you are enjoying your holiday. Shall we go swimming when you get back? Yesterday, we went to the zoo. We saw the penguins being fed. They were very funny. They all lined up to wait for their fish. Then the keeper took them for a waddle around the zoo and everyone took photos.

1. If you want to move text, you don't have to delete it and then type it again in the new place. You can do it like this instead.

First, select from the word "Shall" down to the end of the next line.

Then move the pointer back to here.

2. Select the text as shown in the top picture above but, before lifting your finger, move the pointer back to the question mark.

I hope you are enjoying your holiday. Yesterday, we went to the zoo. We saw the penguins being fed. They were very funny. They all lined up to wait for their fish. Then the keeper took them for a waddle around the zoo and everyone took photos.

I didn't like the monkeys at all. One of them threw a banana right at me. All I did was say "Hello". Perhaps he thought I was hungry.
Shall we go swimming when you get back?

The pointer

The words in their new position.

3. Press Ctrl and X. The words disappear. Put the pointer where you want them to be and click. Press Ctrl and V. They reappear.

Adding pictures

Click on the WordPad bar.

1. Open Paint and draw a picture. Use the select tool to draw around it. Press Ctrl and C. Click on the WordPad bar below the screen.

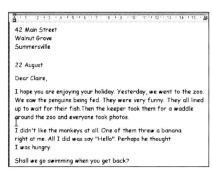

2. Your words reappear. Click where you want to put the picture. It is best to click in a space between lines, as shown above.

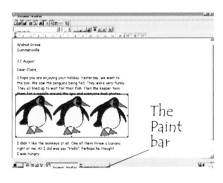

The Paint bar

3. Press Ctrl and V. Your picture appears. To go back to Paint to draw and add another picture, click on the Paint bar shown above.

42

Checking the fit

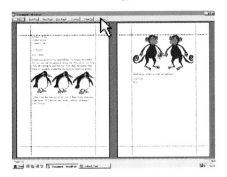

Click on Close to go back to WordPad.

This letter has gone onto a second page.

1. Before you print out, follow all the steps on page 30. In step 4, click on Portrait. In Print Preview, you may need to click on "Two pages" or "Next page" at the top of the screen, if your letter is a long one.

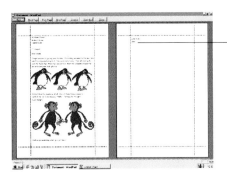

The words are smaller now but the letter still goes onto two pages.

2. You might want to fit a letter like this onto one page. There are two ways of doing this. One is to make the words smaller (see page 40). Then, go back to Print Preview to see if this has helped.

Drag the arrow to shrink the picture.

3. Another way is to make the pictures smaller. In WordPad, click on a picture, then drag one of the squares to shrink it.

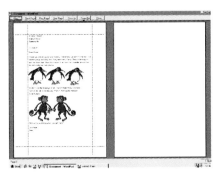

Now you could make your words or pictures a little bigger again.

4. Go back to Print Preview and check the fit again. You may need to change the size of your pictures or words several times to make the letter fit exactly how you want it.

43

Saving your work

You will sometimes want to save what you have been doing in Paint or WordPad. This may be because you want to continue working on a picture or some writing another time. Or, you may want to keep something so you can print out more copies of it later. Before you can save your work, you have to set up a folder, where it can be stored.

Set up a folder

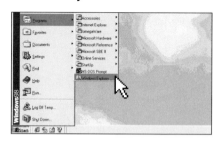

1. To set up a folder, click on Start, move up the list to Programs, then across to the next list. Click on Windows Explorer.

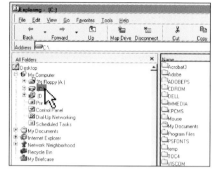

2. A big box appears, split into two lists. In the list on the left, look for a symbol with the letter C beside it. Click on the letter or symbol.

3. Click on File near the top left-hand corner of your screen. Move the pointer down to New and then across to Folder. Click.

4. A new folder appears in the list on the right. Decide what you want to call it. It is best to use your name, for example, "Sam's folder".

5. Type the words on the keyboard. Press the Return key. Click on the cross in the top right-hand corner to close Windows Explorer.

Design a letterhead

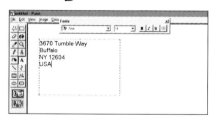

1. A letterhead is your own address at the top of a letter. In Paint, click on the text tool and draw a large text box. Type your address.

2. Use the fonts box to make the address the style and size you like. Decorate it. Draw around it with the select tool. Press Ctrl and C.

3. Open WordPad. Press Ctrl and V. Your letterhead appears. To start writing, click outside, on the right of the box. Then press Return.

44

Internet link: For a link to a website where you can try a technology trivia game, go to **www.usborne-quicklinks.com**

How to save

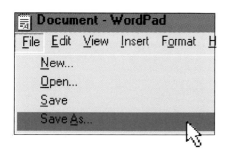

1. To save something, for example your letterhead, click on File at the top left of your screen. Click on Save As in the list.

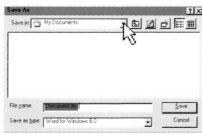

2. A box appears, similar to this one. Now you need to find your folder and give your work a title. Click on the arrow shown above.

3. A list appears. Click on the letter C or its symbol in the list. The screen will change and a list of folders will appear.

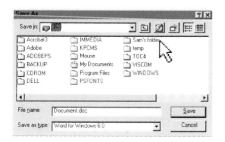

4. Look for your folder in the list. Double click on it. If there is a scroll bar below the list, you may need to drag it to see your folder.

5. Your folder appears at the top of the box, ready for your work to go into it. Put the pointer in the box by File name and double click.

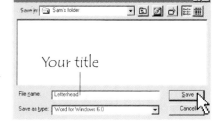

6. On the keyboard, type a title for your work. It appears in the box. Click on Save. The box disappears and your work is saved.

If you design and save a letterhead, you can use it for every letter you write.

To find out how to keep saving your letterhead and using it over and again, see page 47.

Zandberglaan 44
7689 JB Groningen

27 Rue des Glaces
Belleville
92300 St Denis

VIA MARGHERITA 9
76201 BOLOGNA

Switching off

Before you can switch off your computer, you have to close any programs, such as Paint or WordPad, that are open. Then you have to shut down the computer in a certain way. If you forget to do this and just switch off, your computer may not work normally when you switch it back on. Find out below how you can get ready to switch off.

Crashing

There are times when computers seem to "freeze" and you can't make them do anything. This is called a computer crash. Sometimes you can't even close programs and shut down. If your computer crashes, you will need to ask someone to help you sort out the problem.

Closing programs

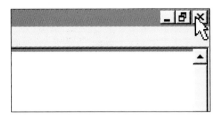

1. The easiest way to close Paint or WordPad is to click on the cross at the top right of the screen. Save your work first if you want to.

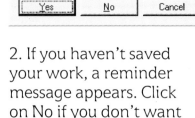

2. If you haven't saved your work, a reminder message appears. Click on No if you don't want to save, on Yes if you do.

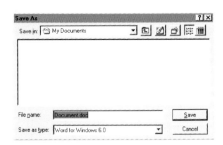

3. If you click on Yes, a box appears, similar to this one. Follow steps 2 to 6 of How to save on page 45. Then the program will close.

Shutting down

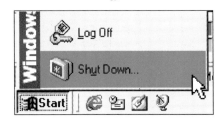

1. When you've closed your programs, the screen will look like the one described on page 3, step 2. Click on Start, then on Shut Down.

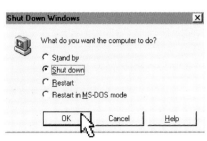

2. A box appears. Click on OK or Yes. Wait for the screen to go black, or for a message telling you it is safe to turn off the computer.

3. Different computers switch off in different ways. Ask someone to tell you which buttons to press the first time you do this.

Finding your work

If you have saved your work and then closed the program you were using, you will need to know how to find the work again later. This page tells you how to do this. First, you need to open the program you were using when you saved your work. Remember, you use Paint mainly for drawing pictures and WordPad for doing a lot of writing.

The last few things you saved are listed here.

1. Click on File at the top left. Look for the title of your work in the list. If you see it, click on it. It will come up on the screen.

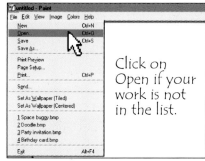

Click on Open if your work is not in the list.

2. If your work is not listed, click on Open near the top of the box. A different box appears. This lets you find your work another way.

Click here first.

Then click here.

3. Click on the arrow near the top of the box. Then click on the letter C in the list. The screen will change to show a list of folders.

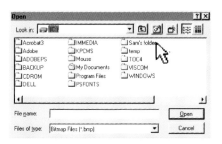

4. Double click on your folder in the list. If you are in Paint, all your Paint titles will appear, if in WordPad all your WordPad titles.

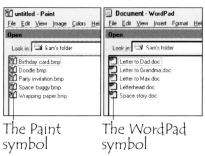

The Paint symbol   The WordPad symbol

5. Paint and WordPad titles have different symbols beside them. Double click on the title you want to see. It will appear on the screen.

Saving again

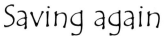

Click here to save.

1. If you want to save your work again later, click on File at the top left of the screen, then on Save as. A box like this one appears.

2. To save only the latest version of your work, click on Save in the box in step 1. Then click on Yes, when this box appears.

Type a new name for your letter before you click on Save.

Or, if you want to keep the earlier version of your work too, for example, your letterhead, you need to rename your latest version.

Index

With thanks to Jessica Bailey, the Butlers, the Brittons and the Twomeys.

Microsoft® Windows® 98 and Microsoft® Windows® 95 are either registered trademarks or trademarks of Microsoft Corporation in the United States and/or other countries. Screen shots reprinted by permission from Microsoft Corporation.

Photographs of computers on front cover and on page 2 reprinted by permission from Hewlett-Packard.